Train Travel

I Talk You Talk Press

CONTENTS

INTRODUCTION

In this book there are five short stories about train travel.
Story 1: The Violin
Story 2: Mrs Wilson Takes a Trip
Story 3: The Last Train
Story 4: Who are You?
Story 5: Owen's Great Adventure

1. THE VIOLIN

Adam opened his eyes and looked out of the train window. The Italian countryside was beautiful in the late afternoon sun. He looked at his watch. It was 4:00pm.

We will arrive in Florence in thirty minutes, he thought.

He looked around the train. There was a young woman sitting opposite him. She was asleep. She was holding a handbag, and on the seat next to her, there was a violin case.

A businessman was sitting on the other side of the train. He was reading a newspaper. A young man was listening to his iPod and reading a book.

Adam was a student from Malaysia. He was travelling alone around Italy for two weeks. He looked out of the window again, and thought about his trip.

My trip has nearly finished, he thought. *I only have three more days before I go back home. It has been a great holiday. I've visited many cities. I've taken many photographs. I've visited many museums. But what shall I do tonight? First, I have to find a cheap hotel when I arrive in Florence. After that…*

There was a magazine on another seat. Adam stood up and picked it up. It was an events magazine.

There was a large advertisement for a concert.

---Stefano Ferrero in Concert!---

In the photograph, a man was holding a violin and there was an orchestra behind him.

Adam looked at the date and time of the concert.

---12th July, 8:30pm---

2

That's tonight! thought Adam. *I'd like to go. I haven't been to any concerts or cultural events on this trip yet.*

He looked at the price of a ticket.

---*80 Euros*---

80 Euros! he thought. *That's too expensive!* He closed the magazine. *I'll go for a walk around Florence. That's free.*

The train slowed down and stopped at a station.

Suddenly, the woman woke up. She looked around. She looked out of the window at the station sign.

She said something in Italian. The train doors were starting to close. She picked up her handbag and ran off the train.

"Wait!" shouted Adam. "You left your violin!"

But it was too late. The doors closed and the train started to move.

Adam looked at the violin. Then he looked around the train. The businessman was still reading the newspaper, and the young man was still listening to his iPod and reading his book. Adam picked up the violin case. There was an address on it.

I can take it to the woman's house, he thought.

He looked up the address on his smartphone. It was not too far from the station.

I can get off at the next stop, and get the train back to that station. I have a map. It is a nice day. I can walk, he thought.

At the next station, he got off the train and went to the other platform. After ten minutes, the train came. He took the train back to the station. He got off the train, walked out of the station, and looked at the map on his smartphone.

It's about a ten-minute walk, he thought. *I can take the violin to the woman, then, I can take the train to Florence. It will still be early evening when I arrive there.*

He started walking. He looked around him. The houses were very big. The houses had large gates, and some houses had security cameras. He looked at his map again and stopped outside a house.

This is it, he thought.

He looked at the house. It had a high gate, and a large garden with many flowers and trees. The house looked like a small palace, and there was a Ferrari outside the door.

Wow! A Ferrari! Does the woman live here? he thought. *She must be very rich.*

Then, he heard a voice. He looked through the gates.

He saw the woman from the train. She was walking up and down in the garden. She was talking on a mobile phone, and she was crying. She was speaking Italian, so Adam couldn't understand, but she looked very upset.

The woman ended the call and rubbed her eyes. Then, a man came out of the house.

I've seen his face before, thought Adam. *Where have I seen him?*

The man was shouting at the woman. He looked very angry. The man got into his Ferrari and started the engine. Then he saw Adam.

Adam waved. The man got out of the car and ran to the gates. He said something to Adam in Italian. He sounded angry.

Adam held the violin case up.

"Your friend left this on the train," he said.

The man shouted something in Italian. He started to laugh and shout.

The woman ran to the gate. She started to scream.

"Grazie! Grazie! Thank you! Thank you so much!" she shouted.

The man opened the gate. "Come in! Come in!" he said in English.

The woman hugged Adam. He was very surprised. The man took the violin from him.

They walked thought the garden and into the house. The man and woman were talking, but Adam didn't understand them.

Adam looked around the hallway. There were expensive antiques and paintings everywhere. They walked into the living room. There was a grand piano next to the window, and a sofa and chairs.

Wow, thought Adam. *This family is very rich!*

"Please, take a seat," said the woman. "I'm Flora. Nice to meet you."

"I'm Adam. Nice to meet you too."

A housekeeper brought coffee and cakes. The man opened the violin case. He picked it up and started to play it.

Wow. He is a professional, thought Adam. The sound was beautiful.

"Please, have some coffee and cake," said Flora. Adam drank some coffee.

"Thank you so much," she said to Adam. "This is Stefano Ferrero. He is one of Italy's top violinists. He has a concert in Florence tonight."

Adam thought about the magazine. *That's why I know his face!* he thought. *He was in the magazine on the train!*

"Are you his wife?" asked Adam.

"No, I am his secretary. This morning, Stefano had some problems with his violin. He was very busy, so I took it to the specialist repairman in the next town. Usually I drive, but the train was quicker. So I took the train. Recently I have been working very hard, so I'm very tired. I fell asleep on the train. The train stopped at my station. I woke up and I panicked. I ran off the train, and I left the violin."

Stefano stopped playing and put the violin down. He looked at Adam.

"Do you live in Italy?" he asked.

"No, I don't. I'm a student from Malaysia. I'm backpacking around Italy for two weeks."

"What plans did you have for today?" asked Stefano.

"I planned to go to Florence, find a hotel and walk around the city," said Adam.

"I'm so sorry. You couldn't do anything today, because of my mistake," said Flora.

"Oh no, it's no problem," said Adam. "It was an adventure for me and I was happy to help."

Stefano and Flora started to talk to each other in Italian. They talked for about ten minutes. Adam didn't understand. He ate a cake and finished his coffee.

Then, Flora looked at him and smiled. "We have a surprise for you," she said.

A few hours later, a very large, expensive black car stopped outside the concert hall in the centre of Florence. The driver got out and opened the car door.

Adam got out of the car. An assistant from the concert hall was waiting for him. She took him into the hall, up the stairs, and into a private box.

"This is your private box, Sir," said the woman. "I hope you enjoy the concert. Please wait here when the concert finishes."

"OK, thank you," said Adam.

Adam looked down. From the box he had a wonderful view of the stage and concert hall.

This is amazing! he thought.

Adam enjoyed the concert. Stefano and the orchestra were

wonderful.

After the concert, the woman came to the box. She took him outside to the car. Adam got into the car and they drove to a restaurant.

"Where are you taking me?" Adam asked the driver.

"You will have dinner with Signor Ferrero and his friends," said the driver.

Adam was surprised. He couldn't speak. The car stopped outside a large restaurant.

Wow! thought Adam. *This looks expensive.*

He walked into the restaurant and sat down. Stefano and his friends came. Stefano told his friends about the violin and Adam. The food was delicious and Adam had a wonderful time.

At the end of the night, Adam was worried. He looked at his watch.

It's 12:30 am, he thought. *I don't have a hotel yet.*

Stefano looked at him. "Are you OK Adam?"

"Yes, I am. I had a wonderful time. Thank you very much. But, I have no hotel yet…"

Stefano smiled. "Don't worry about that. It is arranged. I have to say 'thank you' to you. Thanks to you, I could do the concert tonight. You are a very kind young man."

"Oh, I didn't do anything special," said Adam.

"Yes, you did. You were very kind and I am very grateful. Thank you."

Adam asked someone to take a photograph of him and Stefano. He asked Stefano for his autograph.

This is a great story to tell my family and friends, he thought.

He said goodbye and got into the car. After a few minutes, the car arrived at a very large and expensive hotel. It was the top hotel in Florence.

"This is your hotel for the next two nights, Sir," said the driver.

"But I can't pay…" said Adam.

"Signor Ferrero paid for you. Don't worry," said the driver.

Adam checked in and went to his room. It had a bedroom, a bathroom and a living room.

This is very different from the cheap hotels I've been staying in! he thought.

Adam thought about his day. He thought about the woman on the train and the violin. *Travelling is interesting. Anything can happen,* he thought.

He fell asleep quickly that night, dreaming of trains and violins.

2. MRS WILSON TAKES A TRIP

It was almost 9:00am. Mrs Jessie Wilson was standing on the rail platform at Levin, waiting for the train.

Her friend and neighbour, Lizzie Barton, was waiting with her.

"Thank you for driving me to the station," said Mrs Wilson.

"No problem," said Lizzie. "Taxis are so expensive. I hope you have a nice holiday with your son and his family. I'll feed the cats and collect your mail."

"Thank you, Lizzie. Take anything you want from the garden. The tomatoes are almost ripe, so please pick them all and eat them."

"I will," said Lizzie.

A man in a uniform came up to them. "Are you travelling on the Northern Explorer?" he asked.

"Yes, I'm going to Auckland," answered Mrs Wilson. She gave the man her ticket.

"I will take your luggage," said the man. "How many bags do you have?"

"Just one." Mrs Wilson pointed to her suitcase.

The man checked her ticket and put a label on her suitcase.

"The train will be here very soon," he said. He gave her ticket back, and took her suitcase away.

"Do you have everything you need?" asked Lizzie.

"Yes." Mrs Wilson counted her small bags. "I have my handbag, my lunch and my knitting bag.

The train arrived at the station. Lizzie hugged Mrs Wilson. "Have a wonderful time. Please say 'hello' to Neil and his wife for me."

"Thank you Lizzie. I'll send you a postcard."

Mrs Wilson got on the train and found her seat. There was a

woman sitting next to the window. Mrs Wilson sat down in her seat next to the aisle.

She put her bags on the floor by her feet, and relaxed. She was pleased that someone was sitting next to her. Mrs Wilson liked to talk to new people.

The train started moving. Mrs Wilson could see Lizzie standing on the platform. She waved to Lizzie, and Lizzie waved back. The train moved faster, and soon they were out of the town and were speeding along the seacoast. The train had very big windows and Mrs Wilson could see the houses and farms clearly as they passed by.

"This seat is very comfortable," she said to the woman sitting next to her. "I usually take the bus to Auckland. But my son Neil said to me, 'Why not take the train Mum?' I told him, 'It's too expensive.' So he paid for my ticket. He's a very good son. He works in a bank. He has three children now. I haven't seen the baby yet. So I'm going to visit."

The woman next to her was looking out the window. She didn't answer.

Maybe she's foreign, thought Mrs Wilson. *Maybe she doesn't speak English. This train is very popular with tourists. Maybe she's a tourist.*

Mrs Wilson tried again. She spoke very slowly. "My name is Jessie Wilson. I live in Levin. Where are you from?"

The woman still didn't say anything.

Perhaps she can't hear me, thought Mrs Wilson. "Where are you from?" she said loudly.

The woman didn't turn her head.

Oh, well, thought Mrs Wilson. *It would be nice to have someone to talk to. But you can't have everything. I have my knitting and my book.*

Mrs Wilson enjoyed the view for a while. Then she took out her knitting. The woman next to her was still looking out the window.

She must be asleep, thought Mrs Wilson. *She's a strange person. Who is she? Why is she on the train?*

The woman had long blonde hair. She was wearing a black jacket, a short purple skirt and high black boots with gold buckles down the sides.

The train reached Ohakune at lunchtime.

Almost halfway to Auckland, thought Mrs Wilson.

About 15 minutes after the train left Ohakune station, it stopped. There was an announcement.

--- *"We are very sorry. There will be a short delay. Please stay in your seats."*--

Mrs Wilson looked out the window. The railway line was next to the road. On the road she could see some police cars.

What's the problem? she thought.

Just then, she felt something very hard pushing into her ribs. Mrs Wilson looked down.

The woman next to her was holding a gun against Mrs Wilson's body.

"Stand up," whispered the woman. "We are going to get off the train."

"OK," said Mrs Wilson. "Just let me get my bags. I haven't eaten my lunch yet."

The woman looked puzzled. She pushed the gun harder against Mrs Wilson's ribs. "Don't talk so loudly," whispered the woman. "People will hear you. Move! Or I will shoot you!"

Mrs Wilson was calm. "That would be a very silly thing to do, dear. Just wait. I'm happy to go with you, but I want my bags."

She picked up her knitting, her lunch and her handbag.

She stood up and started walking along the aisle. The woman held her arm tightly and pushed the gun into her back.

"Hey," said another passenger. "They told us to stay in our seats. You must sit down."

The woman pressed the gun harder into Mrs Wilson's back.

"Ow!" said Mrs Wilson. "That hurt!"

"Are you OK?" asked one of the passengers.

"Yes. I just twisted my knee. I understood the announcement, but I really must go to the bathroom. I have trouble walking. So this kind woman is helping me."

At the end of the carriage, the woman with the gun pushed Mrs Wilson towards the door. The door had a window. Mrs Wilson looked out. There were many policemen walking along the outside of the train. There were policemen with dogs and two groups of men, dressed in black, carrying rifles.

"My goodness," said Mrs Wilson. "You must be a very dangerous criminal! Look! They even have the armed offenders squad here."

"Shut up!" said the woman. "You are a stupid woman. Why aren't you frightened? Open the door!"

Mrs Wilson opened the door of the carriage.

"Now put your hands in the air!"

The police on the ground were very surprised to see a small white-haired woman standing in the door of the train with her hands in the air. In one hand she had a handbag, and in the other hand she was holding a brightly coloured knitting bag and a supermarket bag.

Behind her they could see a blonde-haired woman wearing a black jacket.

"That's her!" shouted one of the policemen. "That's Sylvia Montenaga!"

"If you come close to us, I will shoot her!" shouted the woman. "Move back!"

"Move back!" shouted the leader of the policemen. "Don't take any actions! She has a hostage!"

The police moved a little way back.

"Get down from the train," said the woman.

"Oh. Your name's Sylvia? My sister's called Sylvia. I'm Jessie. Well, Jessica, but everyone calls me Jessie. I think Sylvia's a much nicer ......"

"Stop talking!" shouted Sylvia. "Get off the train! Now!"

"Can I put my hands down, please?" asked Mrs Wilson. "I can't climb down without holding onto the railing."

"OK," said Sylvia. She put her arm around Mrs Wilson's neck and pressed the gun against her head. "Now move!"

The policemen were very shocked. They watched Mrs Wilson try to climb out of the train. Sylvia Montenaga was much bigger and heavier, and she was pressed up against Mrs Wilson's back. The bottom step was about a metre above the ground.

"I'll have to jump," said Mrs Wilson. It was hard for her to speak with Sylvia's arm around her neck.

"No!" shouted Sylvia. But it was too late. Mrs Wilson jumped forward. She landed on the ground with Sylvia on top of her. The gun flew through the air. A policeman ran forward and picked it up. Then some policemen pulled Sylvia off Mrs Wilson and took her away.

Other policemen ran forward. "Are you OK?" they asked Mrs Wilson.

Mrs Wilson couldn't speak for a few moments. Then she said. "Yes, I'm fine."

The policemen helped her to stand up.

"Will you come with us please?" asked one of the policemen. "We will ask a doctor to check you. And we need to ask you some questions."

"I have a question first," said Mrs Wilson. "Who is she? Why were you looking for her on the train?"

"Her name is Sylvia Montenaga. She is a drug smuggler. We were chasing her in Wellington. We looked everywhere. Then we found a dead woman near the railway station. Someone had shot her. Her family said she was planning to catch the train to Auckland. So we guessed Sylvia had killed the woman and stolen her ticket. Now please come along with us."

"My bags," said Mrs Wilson. "I need my bags."

"I have them here," said a young policewoman. She showed Mrs Wilson. "See, I have three bags."

She gave the three bags to Mrs Wilson.

Mrs Wilson looked in her supermarket bag. "My sandwiches!" she said. Mrs Wilson sounded very upset.

The policemen were surprised. "What's wrong?" asked the policewoman.

"I haven't had lunch yet. And my sandwiches! They are all squashed. Really! That Sylvia Montenaga is not a nice person. She ruined my lunch!"

3. THE LAST TRAIN

Andrew looked out of the shinkansen bullet train window. The train was travelling very fast. Andrew was a tourist from Jamaica. He was travelling around Japan. He planned to spend a few days in Shikoku, with his Canadian friend, Phillip. Philip was teaching English in Takamatsu.

This train is so fast, he thought. *It's very comfortable and convenient.*

The train started to slow down. Andrew looked around. He heard the announcement:

---Next stop, Okayama. Okayama---

This is my stop, he thought. He picked up his backpack and bag, and stood next to the door. His bag was very heavy. He put it on the floor. After a few minutes, the train slowed down and stopped. The door opened and he got off.

I have to hurry, he thought. *My train to Takamatsu is the last train. It leaves very soon. Where do I go?*

He looked around and saw a sign for train transfers.

Ah, this is it, he thought. He walked quickly through the station. He arrived at the transfer gate.

Oh, I need to put my ticket through the machine to transfer, he thought. He opened his bag.

Where is my ticket?

Andrew looked through his bag. He couldn't find his ticket.

Maybe I left it on the train. Did I drop it?

Andrew looked and looked and looked, but he couldn't find his ticket.

13

What time is my train? he thought. He looked at the board. *Oh no! I only have one minute!*

He took everything out of his bag and put it on the station floor. The ticket was at the bottom of his bag.

It's here! he thought. He put the ticket through the ticket machine and ran down the steps to the platform. The train doors closed and the train started to move.

Oh no! I've missed it! thought Andrew. He looked around. It was nearly midnight. There were no other passengers on the platform. He went back up the steps and said to the station man, "Excuse me, are there any more trains tonight?"

The station man shook his head. "No, there aren't any. The station will close now."

"OK, thanks," said Andrew.

He walked out of the station and called Phillip.

"Hey, where are you?" asked Phillip. "Are you on the train?"

"No, I'm not. I missed the last train at Okayama."

"That's terrible! What are you going to do?" asked Phillip.

"I don't know. I can't come to Takamatsu tonight. I'll have to stay in Okayama. I'll call you in the morning."

"OK, take care," said Phillip.

Andrew put the phone in his pocket. He looked around.

Then, a man behind him said, "Excuse me."

Andrew turned around. "Hi," he said.

"I'm sorry, but I heard you talking on the phone. Did you miss the last train to Takamatsu?"

"Yes, I did," said Andrew.

"I can help you find a hotel," said the man.

"Really? Thank you. That's so kind of you," said Andrew.

"No problem," said the man. "I'm Hiroshi. Nice to meet you."

"I'm Andrew. Nice to meet you too."

"Where are you from?"

"I'm from Jamaica," said Andrew. "Your English is excellent."

"Oh, thank you. I studied in New Zealand for a year," said Hiroshi.

Andrew looked at Hiroshi. He was about twenty-five years old and he was wearing a suit.

"I'm sorry, are you on your way home from work? You must be very tired. I'm sorry to trouble you."

"It's no problem. I've just finished work," said Hiroshi.

They walked into a hotel. Hiroshi spoke to the receptionist. The hotel was full. They went to another hotel. That was full too.

"I'll have to sleep on a bench, or in a park," said Andrew.

"No, no, no. You can't do that," said Hiroshi. "I have an idea."

Hiroshi took his phone out of his pocket and made a phone call. Then, he looked at Andrew and smiled. "Come on," he said. "You are coming home with me! You can stay with my family!"

"What? No, I can't do that!" said Andrew.

"Of course you can! My parents are waiting. My father likes talking to people from other countries. My house is only fifteen minutes on foot. Come on."

Fifteen minutes later, they were standing outside a large traditional Japanese house.

"Wow!" said Andrew. "Look at the garden!" There was a bridge and many small pine trees in the garden. There were small lights around the walls.

"My father is retired, so he spends a lot of time in the garden," said Hiroshi.

They went into the house. Hiroshi's mother and father were waiting for them.

"Welcome!" they said.

"I'm so sorry," said Andrew. "It's so late, and..."

"No it's not. It's Friday night. We always stay up late on Friday nights," said Hiroshi's father.

They took their shoes off and went into the guest room.

Andrew looked around. There were tatami mats on the floor and sliding paper screens on the windows. There was a beautiful painting of flowers and birds too.

"This is so beautiful," said Andrew.

"Have you ever been in a Japanese house before?" asked Hiroshi.

"No, I haven't," he said. "I wanted to visit a Japanese house, but I don't have any Japanese friends. I've been staying in hotels. This is really special."

"Please, sit down," said Hiroshi's mother.

They had tea and rice cakes. Hiroshi's father asked Andrew many questions about Jamaica. Andrew asked many questions about Japan.

"What are you going to do tomorrow?" asked Hiroshi's mother.

"I'm going to get the train to Takamatsu. My friend teaches English there," said Andrew.

"We will take you by car," said Hiroshi's father.

"Oh no, you can't do that. That's too much trouble for you. It's very far…"

"It's no trouble. Tomorrow is Saturday. And it's a beautiful drive across the Seto Inland Sea. We can have a day trip. We can take you and your friend for lunch."

"Really? But…"

"It's no problem, Andrew. My mother and father enjoy talking to people. We can all go together. I haven't been to Takamatsu for a long time. It will be fun," said Hiroshi.

"Thank you so much," said Andrew.

Hiroshi's mother looked at the clock. "It's two thirty am!" she said. "You must be tired Andrew. I'll bring your futon."

Hiroshi's mother brought a futon for Andrew. He slept very well that night.

The next morning, after breakfast, they all got into the car. It was a beautiful day.

Andrew took many pictures of the sea. When they arrived in Shikoku, his phone rang.

It was Phillip. He told Phillip his story.

"You were so lucky, Andrew!" said Phillip. "I was worried about you."

"Yes, I am very lucky," said Andrew. "Oh, and my friends will take us out for lunch."

"Really? Great! I'm looking forward to meeting your new friends," said Phillip. "You are having a great adventure in Japan, Andrew!"

"Yes, I am. Last night, when I missed the train, I was very worried. But now, I'm glad I missed the train. I could stay in a traditional Japanese house, and the view from the bridge was amazing in the daytime. But best of all, I made some very nice new friends! I've invited Hiroshi and his family to visit me in Jamaica next year. They said yes!"

4. WHO ARE YOU?

David was on the train from Prague to Brno. He was looking out the window at the small villages. The country was very beautiful. Sometimes he even saw a castle! He took many photographs. He felt very excited. He planned to stay in a youth hostel in Brno and spend a few days cycling. He looked at his watch.

It's one o'clock. Two hours before the train arrives in Brno. I should eat something, thought David.

He opened his backpack and took out the ham sandwiches he bought in Prague railway station. They tasted very good, but when he finished them, he felt thirsty. He took out his water bottle. It was empty.

I'll go to the dining car and have a beer, he thought. *Czech beer is excellent.*

The dining car was busy. David looked around. There were no empty tables.

I will have to ask someone if I can share with them, he thought.

He saw a young man sitting alone at a table for two. He had a glass of beer in front of him and he was reading a book. *I'll ask him,* thought David.

He walked over to the table. "Excuse me. There are no free tables. Is it OK if I join you?"

The young man didn't look up. "Sure," he said.

"Thank you," said David.

He sat down at the table. The young man looked up from his book and smiled. David felt dizzy. *What is wrong with me?* he asked himself. *Am I sick? Am I dreaming? Is it a mirror? I am looking at myself!*

David shook his head. The young man on the opposite side of the table was wearing a suit. David looked down at his clothes. *I am wearing jeans and a T shirt. It's not me but....*

"Who are you?" asked David.

The man opposite him said something at the same time. He looked very surprised and he was shaking his head. David didn't understand what he said.

The man said, "No, sorry. You speak English. Who are you?"

David said, "Who are you?"

"I'm Robert. Robert Horak. You surprised me. You look just like me!" Robert laughed.

"No!" David laughed too. "You look just like me! I'm David Bateman. I'm Australian."

David and Robert didn't speak again for a few moments. They just looked at each other. Robert picked up his glass of beer and finished it very quickly. He looked pale and shocked.

It's so strange, thought David. *Robert's hair is a little shorter than mine, and he is wearing a suit. But otherwise it is like looking in a mirror.*

Robert stood up. "It's a special day when you meet your twin. I think I will have another beer. Do you want one?"

"Yes, please!" said David.

Robert came back with two beers and put one of the glasses in front of David.

David picked up his beer. "Thank you." The beer was good and David was thirsty.

"I said 'It's a special day when you meet your twin'. It was a joke. But we must be from the same family. We look so much alike," said Robert. "You said you were Australian?"

"Yes," answered David. "But when I was eighteen, I found out that I was born in this country."

"Bateman is not a Czech name." Robert was puzzled.

"No. My mother died in Australia when I was about six months old. A couple called Stella and George Bateman had no children. They became my mother and father. Then when I was eighteen, they told me everything they knew about my real mother. It wasn't very much. She went to Australia from the Czech Republic. She got sick and died. The police and the government tried to find some family in Australia or the Czech Republic. They couldn't find anyone. Stella and George Bateman couldn't have children of their own, so they took me. 'David' was the name my real mother gave me. My parents liked the name, so they didn't change it."

"I understand," said Robert. "So why did you come here? Are you looking for your family?"

"No," said David. "That's impossible. I have no information. But my parents said to me 'You should see your home country'. They gave me an air ticket and a train pass as a graduation present."

"You have just graduated too?" Robert was interested. "I finished university last month. What was your major?"

"Uh, physics," answered David.

"Me too."

"If you don't mind me asking," said David. "Why are you wearing a suit?"

"I went to Prague for a job interview at a technical university."

"Do you think you will get the job?" asked David.

"No, I won't get the job. I don't want to think about it. Let's talk about something else," answered Robert.

David and Robert drank their beers and chatted. They liked the same kind of music, the same movies and they even played the same sports.

"We must be about the same age," said David. "When's your birthday?"

"I'm twenty-two. My birthday is September seventeenth."

David said nothing. He just looked at Robert. Robert looked at David. After a few seconds, Robert said very quietly, "Is that your birthday too? I don't know how or why, but we are twins."

"I think so too," said David. "I think we must be twins. But this is so strange."

"I think I understand. I grew up with my grandparents," Robert said. "They told me that my father died before I was born, and that my mother died when I was very young. They talk about my father all the time, but they never talk about my mother. What did your parents, the Batemans, tell you?"

"They told me my mother died when I was six months old, and they told me her name. It was Ursula Novak."

Just then there was a train announcement.

--- *"We will soon be arriving at Brno railway station."*---

Robert jumped up. "Come on," he said. "Where's your bag?"

"I have a backpack. It's in the other carriage."

Robert and David hurried back to the carriage and took David's backpack.

The train stopped at Brno station and they got off.

"We'll take a bus," said Robert.

"A bus? Where?" David was puzzled. Robert was pulling him along. He seemed excited.

Robert stopped. He turned to face David.

"The only thing I know about my mother is that her name was Ursula Novak. I am taking you to meet our grandparents."

David and Robert were now outside the railway station. They argued.

"I can't just go to these people's house!" said David.

"Yes you can. They are your grandparents!"

"But they don't know me."

"No. Maybe they saw you when you were a baby. But it will be a wonderful surprise for them," said Robert. He was very happy.

David was not so sure. "They might not be happy. They never told you anything about me. Anyway they must be quite old. It will be a terrible shock!"

Robert looked thoughtful. "Yes, that's true. I don't want Grandmother to have a heart attack. I have an idea. You can wait outside the house. I will go in and tell them. Come on, let's catch a bus."

After about ten minutes, they got off the bus. It was a short walk to the house. It was an old two-storied house in a quiet street. There was a low stone wall in front of the house.

"Sit here," Robert said to David. "I will come back soon."

He ran up the path to front door and went into the house.

David put his backpack on the ground and sat on the wall. He felt very nervous.

This is crazy, he thought. He waited for a few minutes. Then, the door opened and two people came running down the path towards the street. The small white haired woman got to David first. She hugged him. She was crying. A very tall thin man with a white beard followed her. He picked up David's backpack.

"Come," he said.

Robert was waiting inside the house. "I told you they would be pleased!" he said. "Meet Alice and Vasil. Our grandparents!"

The old man, Vasil, dropped the backpack on the floor. He

opened the door to a living room. Alice, Vasil, David and Robert sat down at a table. Alice sat next to David. She stroked his arm and patted his face.

"Robert explained how you met," said Vasil. "I don't understand. Please tell us about yourself."

David told them about his life in Australia. He told them about his parents.

"I have a very good life," he said. "I have wonderful parents. They told me about my mother, but they didn't know very much about her."

Vasil looked very serious. "When I see you together I am sure that you are Robert's twin brother. Yes, Robert. You were a twin. I am sorry we never told you. It was too painful. We thought you would be angry. It is not a nice story."

Alice spoke for the first time. "No. I think you will both be very angry. But we must tell you.

"We had only one child. A son. His name was Radek. Radek was clever. We wanted him to have a great career. But when he was at university in Prague, he fell in love. The young woman's name was Ursula Novak. He wanted to leave university and marry Ursula. We were very angry. Ursula had no family, and they were very young. There was a terrible argument about it. Radek left this house. He left the university. He took Ursula and they went away. He never spoke to us again." Alice was crying.

Vasil spoke. "About a year later, the police came here. They told us Radek had died. He was working on a farm and there was an accident with a tractor. The shock and pain were terrible for us. We were so upset. We lost our son.

"Then about two months after that, Ursula came to this house. She brought two very small babies with her. She said their names were Robert and David. Twin boys. The babies were born after Radek died. She asked us to help her.

"At first we said 'no'. We blamed her for taking Radek away from us. We blamed her for Radek's death. But the babies were beautiful. We had no son, but we had two grandsons. So we said 'yes, we will help you. We will give you money if you give the babies to us.'"

"She was very unhappy, but she agreed," said Alice. "She had no money. She loved Radek, but he was dead. She loved you both. She stayed here for a few days. She said 'I will go, and you can keep the babies.' Vasil gave her money. Then one night she disappeared. She took one of the babies with her. We searched for her. The police could not help us."

"She went to Australia," said David quietly. "I guess she used the money you gave her. She took me to Australia, but then she got sick and died."

"You both must be very angry with us," said Vasil sadly. "We did a terrible thing. And then, Robert, we didn't tell you. But believe me. Alice and I have felt very bad ever since Ursula ran away from here. We are very sorry."

Robert and David looked at each other. "It's very sad," said Robert.

"Yes it is," said David. "Poor Ursula. But I was lucky. I have a wonderful family. I have a good life. And Robert and I found each other."

"God is good," said Alice taking one of Robert's and David's hands.

"Yes," said Robert laughing. "God is very good! He is also very clever!"

Everyone looked at him.

"I made a mistake about the job interview day. I thought the interview was today. But it was yesterday! So I missed it. I didn't have the interview. So I was on the train at lunchtime. That was very lucky! I could meet David!"

5. OWEN'S GREAT ADVENTURE

Owen Moore was watching the television in the living room. He was watching a documentary about Niagara Falls. In the programme, the presenter was travelling to Niagara Falls by train.

Owen looked at his father. "Dad, I want to go to Niagara Falls."

His father was reading. He looked up from his book. "Niagara Falls? It's very far from Ottawa."

"But I want to go. It looks amazing. Can we go? It's summer vacation. I have no school. Let's go."

"Owen, your mother and I have to work all summer. We don't have time. Lisa is going to university next year. We can go for a family trip before she starts university. Wait a year." His father started reading his book again.

Next year, thought Owen. *I have to wait a whole year! That's so long!*

"Can I go by myself?" asked Owen.

His father looked at him. "Of course not! You are only twelve!"

The TV documentary finished and Owen went upstairs to his bedroom. He sat on his bed and looked out of the window.

I don't like being young, he thought. *I can't do anything.*

That night, he had a dream. He was at Niagara Falls. He was taking photographs.

He woke up. He looked around his room. *I'm not at Niagara Falls,* he thought. *I'm in my bedroom, in Ottawa.*

He got up and had breakfast. His mother and father were at work. His older sister, Lisa, was still sleeping. He went into the living room and switched on the computer. He found a website for train travel and typed in 'Ottawa to Niagara Falls'.

I can get the train early tomorrow morning, then I can come back the next day, he thought. *It takes around eight hours to get there. How much is it?*

He looked at the price. *It's around two hundred and fifty dollars. Do I have enough money?*

He went up to his bedroom and opened his money box. Every Christmas and birthday, his relatives gave him money. He didn't spend it. He put it in his money box and saved it. *I have three hundred and twenty five dollars,* he thought. *I can buy a train ticket and I have some money for a hotel. I can get a cheap hotel for less than fifty dollars.*

He went downstairs and looked at the website.

I have to pay by credit card, he thought. *I don't have a credit card, but...*

He heard Lisa coming down the stairs. She walked into the living room.

"Lisa, if I give you two hundred and fifty dollars in cash, will you lend me your credit card?" asked Owen.

"Why?" asked Lisa.

"I want to buy some computer games but I need a credit card."

"OK, yeah. But you have to give me the two hundred and fifty dollars in cash now, plus twenty five dollars."

"Why do I have to pay you an extra twenty five dollars?" asked Owen.

"Because I'm doing you a favour. You have to pay ten percent extra," said Lisa.

"OK, OK," said Owen.

Owen got the 275 dollars and gave them to Lisa. She gave him her credit card. She went into the kitchen to make her breakfast.

A few minutes later, Owen was printing his tickets and planning his trip.

Later that evening, he said to his mother and father, "I'm going to stay over at John's house tomorrow night. We are going to watch a movie together."

"OK," said his mother. "Have fun."

Owen smiled. "I will. I'll have lots of fun."

The next morning, Owen got up at 4:30. Very quietly, he got dressed, and went out of the house. His mother, father and Lisa were still asleep.

When he arrived at the station and saw the train, he started to feel very excited.

I'm going to Niagara Falls by train! he thought. *This is so cool!*

He showed his ticket and found his seat. He had a window seat. He looked out of the window as the train left the station. Soon, they were travelling through beautiful green countryside.

Owen smiled. *I'm free!* he thought.

Around five hours later, the train arrived in Toronto. He got off the train and looked around.

Wow! Toronto! *I've never been here before,* he thought. He bought a bottle of cola and a muffin for breakfast. Then, he got on the train for Burlington.

A middle-aged woman was sitting in the next seat. She looked at Owen.

"Are you travelling alone?" she asked.

"Yes, I am," said Owen.

"But you seem very young," she said.

"I'm not so young. I'm just small for my age," said Owen. "I'm sixteen really," he lied.

"Oh, I see," said the woman. "I'm sorry."

Adults always ask questions, thought Owen. *They want to know everything.*

He turned away from the woman and looked out of the window. After a few minutes, he fell asleep.

An hour later, he got off the train and got on a bus.

This is a really long trip, he thought. *But I am nearly there.*

At last, he arrived at Niagara Falls. He got off the bus and got into a taxi.

"To the waterfall please," he said.

He soon arrived at the waterfall. He paid the driver and got out of the taxi. He ran to the waterfall.

Wow! Look at that! That's so cool! he thought. *It's so noisy! Wow! This is better than watching a documentary on TV!"*

Owen took many photographs and walked around. After an hour, he felt hungry. He went into a restaurant and had a hamburger and fries with a glass of cola. It cost 15 dollars.

Owen went out of the restaurant and went for a walk. A few hours later, he looked at his watch.

It's early evening. I should try to find a hotel, he thought. He looked in his wallet.

What? I only have fifteen dollars left? Why? What did I buy?

He thought about the breakfast in Toronto, the taxi ride to the waterfall, and lunch.

Can I get a hotel for fifteen dollars? I'm sure I can get a cheap one. But I'll have to walk into the city. I don't have enough money for a taxi.

Owen was feeling pleased. He was having an adventure. He felt free.

He walked into the centre of the city and looked around. There were many hotels.

That one looks cheap, he thought. He walked into the hotel and asked the receptionist, "Do you have any rooms available?"

"I'm sorry, we don't," said the receptionist. She looked at him closely.

"Are you alone?" she asked.

"Er, yes," he said.

"Where are you from?"

"Ottawa."

"OK, could you just sit here in the lobby? Let me check the rooms again," said the receptionist.

Owen sat down on a chair near the entrance. A few minutes later, two police officers walked in.

"Are you Owen Moore?" asked one of the policewomen.

"Yes," said Owen. "Why?"

"Your family in Ottawa called the police. All the police in Niagara Falls are looking for you. Come with us please."

At the police station, the policewoman took Owen into a room with a computer and switched it on. His mother's and father's faces appeared on the screen.

"What are you doing?" shouted his mother.

"I just wanted to take a trip to Niagara Falls," said Owen. "How did you find me?"

"I called John's mother! She said you were not there! Your dad checked the internet history and found your train reservation!" she said.

"I just wanted to have a summer vacation. I wanted to see Niagara Falls," said Owen.

"I told you, we can go next year," said his father. "I can't believe you have done this, Owen. When you get home, we will talk."

"Your parents are very worried," said the policewoman. "You can stay here tonight, and then go home tomorrow."

Owen went into the waiting room and waited while the policewoman talked to his mother and father.

I am in trouble, thought Owen. *But, I had a good time. Where can I go next year?*

On the wall, there was a painting of the Rocky Mountains.

The Rocky Mountains! he thought. *Yes!*

THANK YOU

Thank you for reading Train Travel. (Word count: 7,909) We hope you enjoyed it.

If you would like to read more level 2 graded readers, please visit our website http://www.italkyoutalk.com

Other Level 2 graded readers include
Adventure in Rome
Andre's Dream
A Passion for Music
Christmas Tales
Danger in Seattle
Don't Come Back
Finders Keepers…
Marcy's Bakery
Men's Konkatsu Tales
Salaryman Secrets!
Stories for Halloween
The Perfect Wedding
The House in the Forest
The School on Bolt Street

Trouble in Paris
Women's Konkatsu Tales

ABOUT THE AUTHOR

I Talk You Talk Press is a Japan-based publisher of language textbooks, graded readers and language learning/teaching resources.

Our team is made up of highly experienced language teachers and translators, who have all studied at least one additional language to an advanced level.

This experience enables us to design our materials from the perspective of both the teacher and the learner. We consult with both teachers and language learners when designing our textbooks and graded readers, and test our materials extensively in the classroom before publication.

We are a fast-growing press, and currently publish graded readers for learners of English. We publish new graded readers monthly.